KU-527-086

CONTENTS

BEYOND OUR PLANET

WHEN WE LOOK UP, WE SEE CLOUDS AND SKY, BUT BEYOND EARTH'S ATMOSPHERE LIES THE MYSTERIOUS REALM OF SPACE. FAR FROM OUR PLANET THERE IS A WEALTH OF OTHER PLANETS, STARS AND MANY MORE OBJECTS, FROM ASTEROIDS AND COMETS TO BLACK HOLES.

The Earth is one of eight planets circling, or orbiting, a star we call the Sun. Together they are called the solar system. The Sun is a massive ball of burning gas, hot enough to warm our planet even though it is billions of kilometres away. It is just one of a vast number of stars clustered into our galaxy. The universe is made up of billions of such galaxies and the vast gaps in between objects, which contain nothing but floating dust and gases.

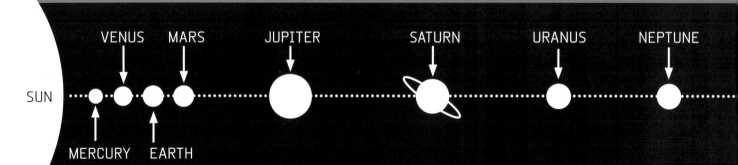

SUN   MERCURY   VENUS   EARTH   MARS   JUPITER   SATURN   URANUS   NEPTUNE

Planets in our solar system range in size from Jupiter, over 300 times bigger than Earth, to Mercury, less than half Earth's size. The four planets closest to the Sun are warm, rocky planets, but the outer planets are giant, cold, spinning balls of gas.

MATHS TALK

An astronomical unit (AU) is the distance from Earth to the Sun, which is 150 million km. But the next nearest star is around 270,000 AU away from Earth. Scientists need larger units called light years to measure the universe. One light year is the distance light travels in one year, or 9,461,000,000,000 km. The universe is around 93 billion light years across!

SPACE

ADVENTURES IN STEAM

Richard Spilsbury

AND

lbooks.co.uk

Published in paperback in Great Britain in 2019 by Wayland

Produced for Wayland by
White-Thomson Publishing Ltd
www.wtpub.co.uk

Series editor: Izzi Howell
Designer: Rocket Design (East Anglia) Ltd
Illustrations: Rocket Design (East Anglia) Ltd
In-house editor: Julia Bird

ISBN: 978 1 5263 0480 3
10 9 8 7 6 5 4 3 2 1

Wayland
An imprint of
Hachette Children's Group
Part of Hodder & Stoughton
Carmelite House
50 Victoria Embankment
London EC4Y 0DZ

An Hachette UK Company
www.hachette.co.uk
www.hachettechildrens.co.uk

Printed in China

Picture acknowledgements:
Julian Baker: 11 and 45l; NASA: 3, 5t, 6, 12, 17t, 17b, 18t, 18c, 18b, 19t, 19c, 20, 22, 23, 24, 26, 27, 29t, 29b, 30b, 35b, 37, 39, 42, JPL-Caltech 5b, 36, 38, Pat Corkery, United Launch Alliance 10, Bigelow Aerospace 21, Dmitri Gerondidakis 31b, ESA, and the Hubble Heritage Team (STScI/AURA) 33, CXC/M.Weiss 34t, JHUAPL/SwRI 34c, JPL-Caltech/UCAL/MPS/DLR/IDA 34b, JPL-Caltech/MSSS 40, 41t, MSFC 43, MarsScientific.com and Clay Center Observatory 45; Shutterstock: iurii cover and title page, RJ Design 7, Jorg Hackemann 8, Everett Historical 9, 28, 30c, 31t, 31c, Andrey Armyagov 14, Harvepino 15, Delpixel 25, AuntSpray 30t, MarcelClemens 32, Belish 35t, solarseven 35c, ESB Professional 41b; Wikimedia: RIA Novosti archive/Alexander Mokletsov / 19b, Jeff Foust44.

All design elements from Shutterstock.

People have been fascinated by and studied space for centuries using ever more advanced technology, from simple telescopes to complex sensors on spacecraft. Some lucky people have even visited and experienced space and had the chance to look down on their home planet from above.

THINKING OUTSIDE THE BOX!

In 1931, Belgian priest and scientist Georges Lemaître proposed the new idea that the universe started with one giant, incredibly hot explosion around 14 billion years ago. He called it the Big Bang. For centuries before this, people widely believed the Earth and everything in space was created by God. In the 1960s, astronomers finally found proof for the Big Bang theory. They detected radiation in the universe that could only be explained as the leftover energy from the explosion.

SCIENCE TALK

Most scientists now agree that the universe was born from a dot of matter far smaller than a pinhead. During the Big Bang, it suddenly expanded outwards. Over millions of years, stars, planets and other objects formed. Scientists know the universe is still expanding today because galaxies are getting further away from Earth and each other.

The galaxy containing our solar system is called the Milky Way because light from stars makes it glow white in the night sky. This is a nearby galaxy of a similar shape to the Milky Way.

GETTING TO SPACE

AFTER CENTURIES OF WONDERING WHAT IT WOULD BE LIKE TO GO TO SPACE, HUMANS STARTED TO MAKE TRIPS THERE FROM THE 1960S ONWARDS. THE CHALLENGES OF REACHING SPACE THEN, AS NOW, WERE ALL ABOUT OVERCOMING THE POWERFUL FORCE OF GRAVITY.

Gravity is the downwards pull towards Earth or other large objects. The pull of gravity on your body, for example, makes you fall if you jump up. Weight is a measure of the force of gravity on any mass (measure of amount of matter). To rise through the air, any aircraft needs to produce a push or thrust upwards greater than its weight to escape gravity's pull. All space missions have produced the massive thrusts needed to lift heavy spacecraft with rocket engines.

The earliest rockets were fireworks made from hollow bamboo pieces packed with gunpowder. Lighting the gunpowder created thrust by shooting hot gases downwards. But the direction of these and later missiles was inaccurate and hard to control. Fast forward to 1926, when scientist Robert Goddard tested the first modern rocket. Goddard's rocket flew for less than three seconds and rose for just under 12.5 m, but demonstrated a technology that would be developed into space rockets.

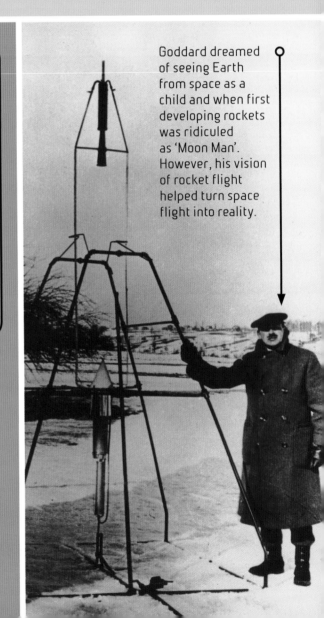

Goddard dreamed of seeing Earth from space as a child and when first developing rockets was ridiculed as 'Moon Man'. However, his vision of rocket flight helped turn space flight into reality.

SCIENCE TALK

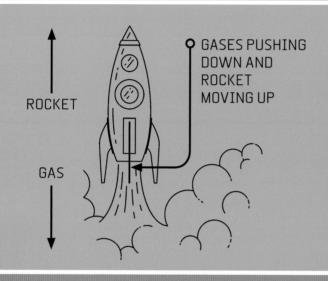

ROCKET

GAS

GASES PUSHING DOWN AND ROCKET MOVING UP

Forces always work in pairs. This is called action and reaction. The action of gases pushing down causes a reaction in the opposite direction and so the rocket is pushed upwards. Goddard's rocket used liquid fuels of gasoline and oxygen in a combustion chamber to achieve lift-off. These provided more controlled thrust than solid fuels of the time because a certain amount could be burnt at a time.

TECHNOLOGY TALK

Goddard improved his rocket design by adding technology. He developed a system of springs and weights that could control the angle of thrust to keep the rocket climbing vertically, a compartment onboard to store scientific instruments and even a parachute that would deploy once fuel had run out to slow the fall of the rocket back to Earth. All of these technologies have been used on space rockets and other flying machines ever since.

MATHS TALK

Solid fuels in Goddard's time gave rockets a two per cent efficiency of converting the energy in fuel into thrust. Goddard's design improvements, including using a specially shaped nozzle for gases, raised the efficiency to 63 per cent. Even today's rockets can rarely achieve more than 70 per cent.

THE FIRST SPACE ROCKETS

DURING THE 1950S, THE SOVIET UNION AND THE UNITED STATES WERE ENEMIES AND WANTED TO OUTDO EACH OTHER. ONE WAY TO SHOW THEIR DOMINANCE WAS TO GET AN ASTRONAUT INTO SPACE BEFORE THE OTHER. THIS COMPETITION BECAME KNOWN AS THE SPACE RACE.

The V2 rocket was controlled by radio signals. These could command motors to move the fins near its base to change the rocket's flight direction so it reached its target accurately.

The rocket had showed its power in the Second World War (1939–1945), when German forces rained down V2 rockets onto London. These liquid-fuelled rockets, launched from Germany, flew 80 km high in the air and then exploded on reaching their target in the UK. The space race happened because each side realised such powerful rockets could carry not only bombs, but also astronauts and spacecraft into space. In 1942, the first German rocket reached space.

After the war, German scientists involved with V2 development teamed up with Russian and US rocket engineers. They helped to build the first space rockets for each side and achieved many more firsts:

 OCT 1957

The Soviet Union launch a new Semyorka rocket to put the first ever satellite, Sputnik 1, in space.

 APRIL 1961

The Vostok-K rocket launches Soviet astronaut Yuri Gagarin to become the first man in space.

MAY 1961

The US Redstone rocket reaches space, but it is not powerful enough to get US astronaut Alan Shepard into orbit.

The liftoff of Apollo 11 on a Saturn V rocket in 1969. The Saturn V rocket was 111 m tall and capable of carrying over 48 tonnes to the Moon. It had a total of ten engines for thrusting it through Earth's atmosphere. It remains the largest space rocket ever built.

THINKING OUTSIDE THE BOX!

The first living things to reach space from Earth were fruit flies in 1947. Ten years later, a dog became the first mammal to leave our planet. Scientists used animals to find out more about the dangers of take-off, high-speed flight and time in space before humans made the trip.

ENGINEERING TALK

The first design for the Sputnik 1 satellite was too heavy for their existing launch vehicle to lift into space, so Russian space engineers reduced its size and weight. Rocket engineers need to carefully consider the weight of the payload (what a rocket carries, from equipment to astronauts) when deciding on the amount of engine thrust a rocket needs.

 FEB 1962

The more powerful Atlas rocket takes US astronaut John Glenn into orbit.

 DEC 1965

Two US astronauts spend two weeks in space.

JULY 1969

A Russian N1 rocket capable of travelling to the Moon explodes on the launch pad, causing the

 JULY 1969

The Saturn V launches the US Apollo 11 mission, whose astronauts complete

REACHING SPACE TODAY

TODAY'S ROCKETS OR LAUNCH VEHICLES COME IN MANY SIZES, DEPENDING ON THE PAYLOAD THEY NEED TO CARRY INTO SPACE. THE LARGEST ARE CALLED HEAVY-LIFT VEHICLES, WHICH CAN CARRY OVER 50 TONNES INTO SPACE, WHEREAS SMALL-LIFT VEHICLES CAN CARRY TWO TONNES AT MOST.

Space rockets are streamlined, with a long, thin shape that helps them move faster through the atmosphere. Objects moving forward through air are pushed back by it and this friction reduces their speed. A streamlined shape reduces the surface area for air to push against. Smooth sides also reduce the friction or air resistance (drag) between air and the rocket's surface.

" MATHS TALK

Only around 1 per cent of a rocket's weight is its payload. Most of the rest is the propulsion system of engines and fuel. For example, the launch vehicle Ariane weighs nearly 800 tonnes at take-off. Of this, 550 tonnes is solid fuel in the boosters, which is used up in the first two minutes of flight, and 175 tonnes is liquid fuel in the main section or stage. That's 90 per cent of its total weight. "

A rocket needs to be tough enough to withstand massive vibrations from the engines while they fire. The inner frame is formed from vertical beams attached to hoops up the length of the vehicle. A smooth metal skin is shaped around this frame. Both are made from strong but lightweight metals such as aluminium alloys. In parts such as the tip and fuel tank, the skin is covered with special carbon fibre heat shields. These reduce the heating of the skin and contents due to friction.

THINKING OUTSIDE THE BOX!

Engineers are designing launch vehicles that are not rockets. One idea is to use a tough balloon filled with helium to lift a small launch vehicle that fires its thrusters around 32 km above Earth. Another idea is to use a maglev train on an upcurved track to launch a type of space plane. Maglevs use the push of magnets against each other to lift trains above tracks, eliminating friction and increasing speed.

PROJECT

Design an aerodynamic rocket to carry a payload of passengers.

- What source of thrust would you use?

- Why might you need tail fins at the end?

- How would you adapt the design to carry a heavier payload?

Many launch vehicles, such as Ariane V, have several stages or parts used for different legs of the journey to space.

SECOND STAGE contains payload such as satellites to deliver in space, and smaller engines and fuel tanks

MAIN STAGE contains giant fuel tanks and thruster engines to get it to space, where it detaches and falls to Earth

BOOSTERS solid fuel rockets that give extra thrust at take-off when a rocket is at its heaviest, before detaching and falling into the ocean

IN ORBIT

SPACE BEGINS AROUND 100 KM ABOVE THE EARTH'S SURFACE. HERE THE FORCE OF GRAVITY FROM EARTH IS WEAKER THAN ON THE PLANET'S SURFACE AND THERE IS SO LITTLE AIR THAT DRAG IS NEGLIGIBLE. SPACECRAFT CAN ORBIT EARTH USING VERY LITTLE THRUST AND FUEL.

Spacecraft control their orbits using small thrusters controlled by computers that nudge them left or right, faster or slower, to ensure they remain at the right speed and height above Earth.

Moving in orbit around Earth relies on gravity. Without it, a rocket would continue outwards on a straight path to outer space. Gravity's pull changes the craft's straight motion into a circular orbit. When you throw a ball hard, it travels straight for longer before arcing to Earth than if you throw it softly. In the same way, spacecraft need to move fast to stop gravity from dragging them back towards our planet. Spacecraft orbit at different heights from Earth to avoid flying too close to each other. Those orbiting closer to Earth need to go fastest, because gravity's pull is stronger.

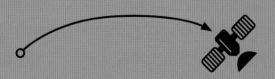

SCIENCE TALK

The force of gravity is so strong that space launch vehicles must reach a speed known as escape velocity to break free of its pull. This is at least 11 km per second (40,000 kph). Once in orbit, a craft must continue to fly at around 27,000 kph to prevent it from being pulled gradually back to Earth.

Spacecraft are not the only man-made objects orbiting Earth. There are also around 370,000 pieces of space junk. These orbiting objects include parts of exploded rockets, disused satellites (see page 14-15), and tools or gloves accidentally dropped by astronauts. Space junk is hazardous because it can fly into, and even punch a hole through, a spacecraft in orbit.

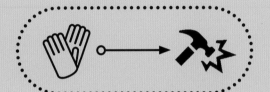

ENGINEERING TALK

Engineers are thinking of solutions to deal with space junk. CleanSpace One is a satellite that hunts down a disused satellite in orbit and uses a mechanical grabber to pick it up. Then both satellites head for Earth. Other ideas include stretching out tough fishing nets between spacecraft to trap junk and using special sensors to spot and track junk movements so that spacecraft can manoeuvre out of its way.

SATELLITES

ON A CLEAR NIGHT, YOU MIGHT SEE A DOT OF LIGHT SLOWLY CROSSING THE DARK SKY. THIS IS MOST LIKELY TO BE AN ARTIFICIAL SATELLITE ORBITING IN SPACE. THERE ARE THOUSANDS OF ARTIFICIAL, OR MAN-MADE, SATELLITES ABOVE EARTH THAT HELP US IN DIFFERENT WAYS.

Some satellites take pictures of Earth to help meteorologists predict weather patterns or allow geographers to make maps. Some take pictures of the Sun, other planets, black holes or distant galaxies to help scientists understand space. Other satellites are used to send TV signals and phone calls around the world.

SCIENCE TALK !

TV and phone signals travel in straight lines, so they can be blocked by mountains or tall buildings. Today, TV signals and phone calls are beamed up to a satellite, which instantly sends them back down to different locations on Earth.

Some satellites are battery powered but most are fuelled by solar panels. Solar panels convert the energy in sunlight into electricity. Satellites have an antenna to send and receive data, such as phone messages and navigation instructions. They have sensors that check they are facing the right way and small rocket thrusters to adjust their direction.

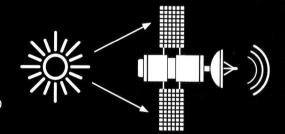

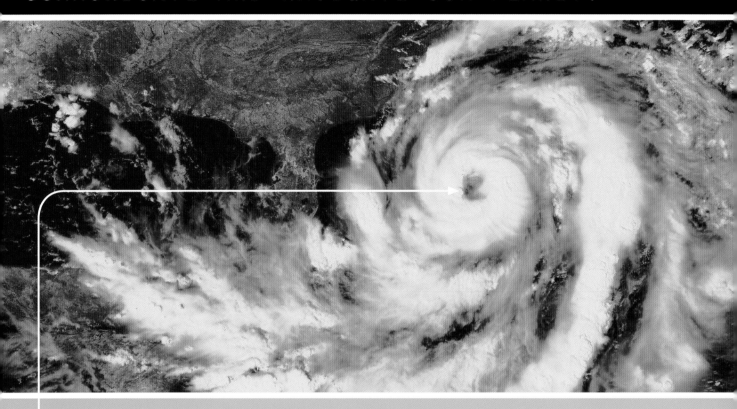

Weather satellites have cameras that take images of clouds and beam them to weather stations on Earth. Meteorologists can use images of a hurricane like this to track its movement and warn people in its path to get to safety.

GPS, or Global Positioning System, satellites help us work out exactly where we are on Earth. Each satellite transmits information about its position and the time. GPS receivers work out how far away each satellite is based on how long it takes for the signals to arrive. They use this information to pinpoint your location.

" MATHS TALK

GPS receivers work by trilateration. Let's say you are on a hill with three satellites in space above. Calculating your distance from satellite 1 tells us you must be located somewhere in the red circle. If you calculate distances from satellites 2 and 3 as well, your location is where the three circles intersect.

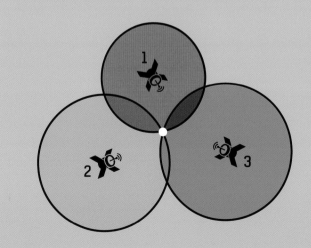

THE MOON

THE MOON IS EARTH'S CLOSEST NEIGHBOUR. IT IS A NATURAL SATELLITE THAT TAKES ABOUT A MONTH TO ORBIT OUR PLANET. IT IS THE ONLY OBJECT IN SPACE THAT HUMANS HAVE SET FOOT ON.

The Moon probably formed about 4.5 billion years ago from debris thrown into space after a vast object crashed into Earth. Unlike Earth, the Moon has a thin, weak atmosphere that cannot protect it from the extreme heat of the Sun, or hold on to the Sun's warmth to stop it freezing at night. It is airless, waterless and lifeless.

SCIENCE TALK

The Moon is much smaller than Earth but it is still large enough to have a gravitational force that affects our planet. The oceans rise and fall up and down the coastline in tides because the Moon's gravity pulls the oceans that are directly below it.

ART TALK

During the Moon's orbit of Earth, the Sun only lights up the side of the Moon that faces towards it. Its appearance changes as the angle at which we see the Moon changes over the month. We may see a crescent, full or new Moon for example.

The first men to walk on the Moon landed there in the Apollo 11 spacecraft in 1969. They had to wear spacesuits to provide them with air and to protect them from the Sun's harmful radiation. They explored the Moon's surface for over two hours, taking film and photos and collecting 22 kg of rocks to study back on Earth.

Gravity's pull on the surface of the Moon is one-sixth of Earth's, which is why astronauts look as if they are bouncing across its surface rather than walking. Without rain, wind, or water to erode astronauts' footprints, they will probably stay there forever!

THINKING OUTSIDE THE BOX!

Astronauts on the Apollo missions left reflectors on the Moon. Scientists bounce a laser off the reflectors and measure how long it takes for the beam to reach Earth again. Using their knowledge of the speed of light, they can work out the distance between the Moon and Earth to within millimetres.

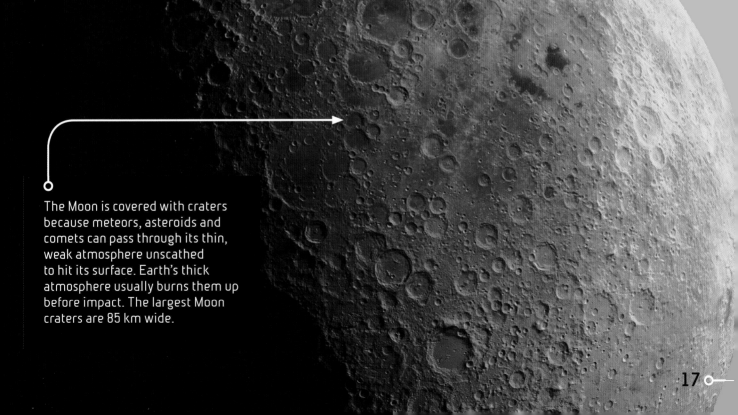

The Moon is covered with craters because meteors, asteroids and comets can pass through its thin, weak atmosphere unscathed to hit its surface. Earth's thick atmosphere usually burns them up before impact. The largest Moon craters are 85 km wide.

MOST OF THE DISCOVERIES AND ACHIEVEMENTS MADE IN SPACE WOULD NOT HAVE BEEN POSSIBLE WITHOUT THE BRAVE MEN AND WOMEN WHO TOOK PART IN THE DARING AND DANGEROUS EARLY FLIGHTS INTO SPACE. THESE ASTRONAUTS TRAVELLED INTO SPACE WITHOUT KNOWING THE RISKS TO THE HUMAN BODY OR IF THEY WOULD EVER RETURN TO EARTH.

YURI GAGARIN (1934-1968)

Yuri Gagarin was a fighter pilot who became an instant worldwide celebrity when he became the first human in space on 12 April 1961. His Vostok 1 spacecraft orbited Earth at 27,400 kph and at his highest point, he found himself about 327 km above Earth. Gagarin died in a crash at the age of 34 after a routine plane flight went wrong.

JOHN GLENN (1921-2016)

John Glenn was the first US astronaut to orbit the Earth. His 1962 flight made the USA a serious contender in the space race with the Soviet Union. In 1988, aged 77, he became the oldest astronaut when he flew onboard the space shuttle *Discovery* (see page 28–29). His mission was to take part in experiments on the effects of living in space on older people.

NEIL ARMSTRONG (1930-2012)

Neil Armstrong was the mission commander on the 1969 Apollo 11 flight, during which he became the first person to walk on the Moon. He famously said, 'That's one small step for (a) man; one giant leap for mankind'. With fellow astronaut Buzz Aldrin, he spent over two hours on the Moon, studying the surface and collecting rocks.

JAMES 'JIM' LOVELL (1928–)

Jim Lovell made four space flights and spent over 700 hours in space but he is most famous as commander of the ill-fated Apollo 13 mission in 1970, which suffered a serious explosion two days into the flight. Lovell and his crew narrowly survived the disaster and, with help from mission control, returned to Earth safely. In the 1995 movie *Apollo 13*, Lovell is played by Tom Hanks.

SALLY RIDE (1951–2012)

On 18 June 1983, Sally Ride became the first American woman to fly in space. She was a crew member on space shuttle *Challenger* missions, using the robotic arm she had helped develop. Back on Earth, she began NASA's EarthKAM project that lets schoolchildren take pictures of Earth using a camera on the International Space Station.

VALENTINA TERESHKOVA (1937–)

Valentina Tereshkova was a Russian parachutist-turned-astronaut. On 16 June 1963, she became the first woman to fly in space. During the 70.8-hour flight, her spacecraft Vostok 6 made 48 orbits of Earth. Soon after lift-off, she had to fix a problem on board after discovering that the settings for re-entry were wrong and would have sent her out into space rather than back to Earth!

THE INTERNATIONAL SPACE STATION

THE INTERNATIONAL SPACE STATION (ISS) IS THE LARGEST SPACECRAFT ORBITING EARTH. ASTRONAUTS AND SCIENTISTS FROM THE USA, RUSSIA, JAPAN AND EUROPE LIVE HERE FOR MONTHS AT A TIME, STUDYING SPACE AND ANALYSING HOW THE HUMAN BODY COPES WITH LIVING THERE.

The ISS was constructed in space from modules that were delivered piece by piece by 40 missions between 1998 and 2011. Its design was based in part on successful earlier space stations, including Skylab and Mir. The ISS is 74 m long and 110 m wide, larger than a football pitch. On a clear night, you can see the ISS from Earth as it is the third brightest object in the sky, after the Sun and Moon.

The ISS orbits the Earth 16 times a day at a height of 320 km above Earth's surface. This vast structure would collapse under its own weight if it moved into Earth's atmosphere and experienced our planet's powerful gravity.

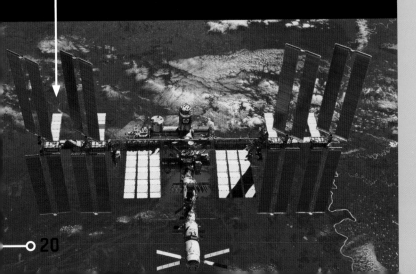

" MATHS TALK

Shapes matter on the ISS. On Earth, structures like bridges use triangles and beams for strength. The framework of the ISS is made up of many such triangular structures and beams. The modules where astronauts live and work are shaped like cans and spheres. On Earth, fizzy drinks come in cans with no corners weak enough to burst under the pressure of the gassy liquid inside. In space, similar shapes can contain the pressurised atmosphere the astronauts need to breathe and survive.

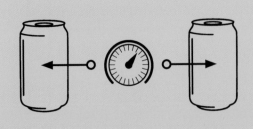

The ISS has about the same amount of room as a five-bedroom house, accommodating a crew of six people, plus visitors. Reaching out from the sides of the space station are arms holding wide, flat solar panels. These are designed to capture enough of the Sun's energy to supply the ISS with ample electricity. The ISS also contains small spacecraft that astronauts can use to escape to Earth in case of an emergency!

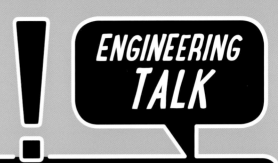

ENGINEERING TALK

Like space rockets, the ISS is made from very strong and lightweight metals such as aluminium, titanium and high-grade steel. Its surface is covered in materials such as Kevlar, the tough stuff used to make bullet-proof vests, to stop the ISS being punctured by debris flying around in orbit (see page 13).

THINKING OUTSIDE THE BOX!

Engineers are using the ISS to test ideas for safe structures for astronauts to live and work in for future space trips to more distant destinations. The Bigelow Expandable Activity Module (BEAM) is an inflatable module that has been tested there. These modules are light and small but after docking with the ISS, they expand to about 4 m long and 3.2 m in diameter.

LIVING IN THE STATION

THE INTERNATIONAL SPACE STATION HAS TO PROVIDE EVERYTHING ASTRONAUTS NEED TO SURVIVE IN SPACE FOR TYPICAL MISSIONS OF 4-6 MONTHS. AS WELL AS ELECTRICITY, CLEAN WATER, FOOD AND AIR TO BREATHE, THEY NEED PROTECTION FROM THE TEMPERATURE EXTREMES IN SPACE: 200°C IN THE DAY TO -200°C AT NIGHT!

Temperatures are kept at a comfortable 21°C on the ISS, and it is filled with air, so astronauts don't need to wear spacesuits inside. Astronauts float around inside the spacecraft instead of walking and have to strap themselves to their beds and toilets to prevent them floating around and crashing into things. They feel weightless because of microgravity (see Science Talk). Astronauts train in microgravity conditions for months before going to the ISS.

In microgravity conditions, it is easy for astronauts to move heavy objects because the objects are weightless too. Astronauts can shift big boxes and heavy equipment with just a touch of their fingers.

SCIENCE TALK

Gravity pulls all objects in the same way, however big or small they are. The reason a stone drops faster than a feather when you drop them is that air resistance makes the feather fall more slowly. In space there is no air, so the astronauts and the space station are falling at the same speed. This makes astronauts float and feel a less than normal pull of gravity, also known as microgravity.

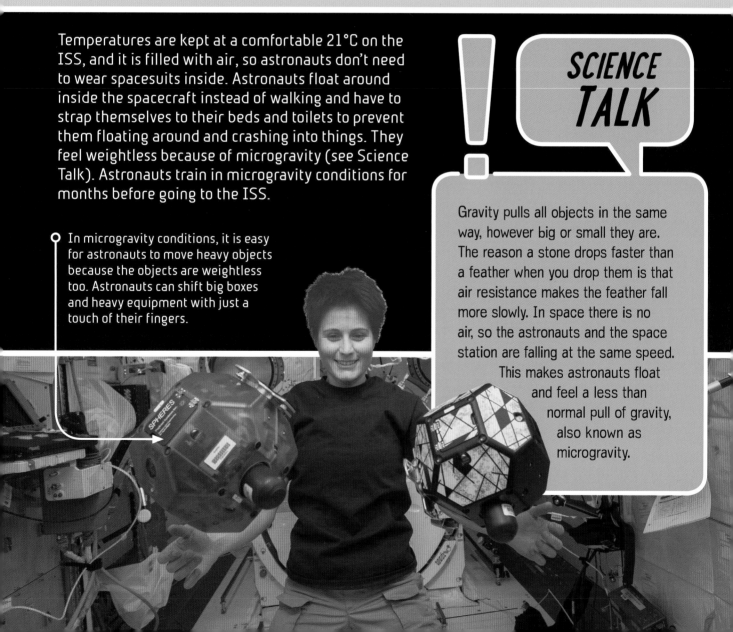

On Earth, muscles and bones work against the force of gravity to support and move our bodies. This helps to keep them strong. To avoid losing bone mass and muscle strength because of microgravity during stays in space, astronauts exercise for two or more hours every day using a variety of gym equipment. Special straps and elastic cords hold them onto treadmills and bikes and create a downward force for them to push against, so the astronauts don't float away as they exercise.

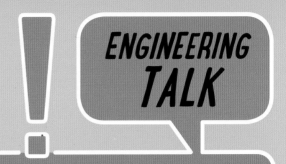

ENGINEERING TALK

It's expensive to transport water from Earth to the ISS so recycling is vital. All waste water is collected, including the astronauts' urine, sweat and moisture from their breath. The waste water is filtered to remove impurities and contaminants to produce clean water that astronauts use to rehydrate dried food, wash or drink.

PROJECT

Design a gym for microgravity conditions in space.

- What sort of machines would you include?
- Why do you need to include machines that encourage weight-bearing exercises such as jogging and climbing?
- How would you make weight-lifting possible in microgravity conditions?

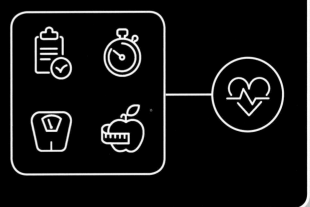

SPACEWALKS

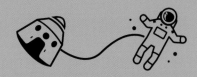

ASTRONAUTS GO ON SPACEWALKS OUTSIDE THE INTERNATIONAL SPACE STATION TO COMPLETE TASKS SUCH AS SETTING UP SCIENCE EXPERIMENTS OR MAINTAINING THE SPACECRAFT. THEY ARE TETHERED TO THE CRAFT BY STRONG SAFETY CORDS TO STOP THEM FLOATING AWAY AND WEAR SPACESUITS FOR PROTECTION.

Spacesuits keep astronauts at a safe, stable temperature using layers of insulation and built-in pipes carrying warm or cool fluids to raise or lower temperatures when needed. The suit contains about 14 layers of different materials. One layer is made of Kevlar to protect the astronaut from space dust and debris hitting them. Another layer is waterproof and yet another is fireproof. A backpack supplies the astronaut with oxygen to breathe and removes the carbon dioxide that they breathe out.

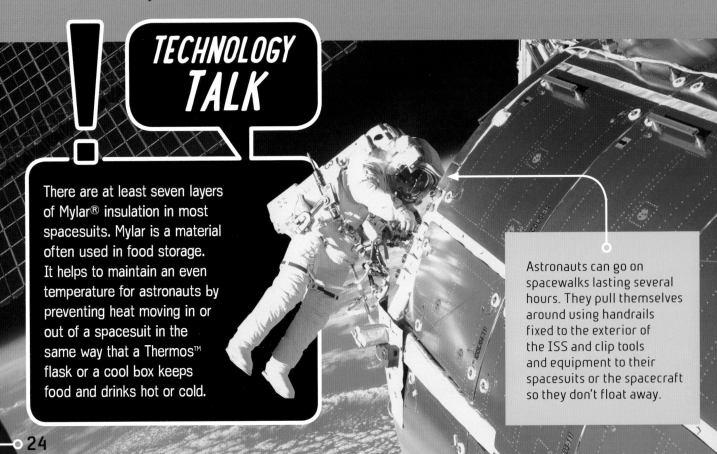

TECHNOLOGY TALK

There are at least seven layers of Mylar® insulation in most spacesuits. Mylar is a material often used in food storage. It helps to maintain an even temperature for astronauts by preventing heat moving in or out of a spacesuit in the same way that a Thermos™ flask or a cool box keeps food and drinks hot or cold.

Astronauts can go on spacewalks lasting several hours. They pull themselves around using handrails fixed to the exterior of the ISS and clip tools and equipment to their spacesuits or the spacecraft so they don't float away.

A device called a Simplified Aid for Extravehicular Activity Rescue, or SAFER, is attached to the back of the astronaut's spacesuit. This is like a jetpack, with several small thruster jets that can be pointed in different directions. The force of gases from a thruster in one direction moves the astronaut in the opposite one. Thrusters help astronauts get back to the ISS if they become separated from the space station.

SCIENCE TALK

On Earth, the weight of air pressing down on us is balanced by air pressure in cavities such as our lungs. As there is no air in space, there is no air pressure and this could cause the gas inside the lungs to expand and burst them. So, one layer of a spacesuit contains air that constantly presses against the astronaut's body to maintain a level of air pressure it can cope with.

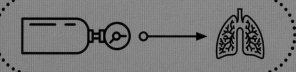

THINKING OUTSIDE THE BOX!

Many of the innovations designed for space have had a big impact on Earth too. The coatings scientists developed for space helmet visors to protect astronauts' eyes from intense sunlight are used to make the lenses in glasses, sunglasses and ski goggles ten times more scratch-resistant. Cameras developed to spot infrared light in space are now used to detect forest fires from long distances.

WORKING IN SPACE

MANY JOBS OUTSIDE THE SPACE STATION AND OTHER SPACECRAFT ARE DONE BY ROBOTS RATHER THAN ASTRONAUTS. SPACEWALKS ARE DANGEROUS AND CAN BE EXHAUSTING FOR ASTRONAUTS. ROBOTS DO NOT GET TIRED, CAN DO TOUGHER WORK IN SPACE CONDITIONS AND ARE REASONABLY EXPENDABLE, UNLIKE PEOPLE.

The heavy duty robot on the ISS is called Canadarm2. This is a 17-m-long robotic arm. It can lift around 116 tonnes, yet is made from tough plastic just 35 cm in diameter. Canadarm2 can move around like a looping caterpillar. It can plug either of its ends into sockets all over the ISS. The sockets supply power and link to joysticks which astronauts use to control the arm's movements.

Canadarm2 is often used to grab visiting spacecraft as they fly nearby and help them dock accurately and safely with the ISS. Astronauts can view and control the exact position of Canadarm2 using colour video cameras at its joints and ends.

ENGINEERING TALK

Robotic arms are made of several long stiff pieces, rather like our arm bones, with joints linking them together that allow the arm to move. In car factories, robotic arms may have just a few parts and simple joints because they are designed to carry out simple movements. Canadarm2 has seven joints, like a human arm, but unlike human elbows and wrist joints, each can rotate fully, allowing a much wider range of movement.

Canadarm2's strength is used to help unload modules from spacecraft docked to the ISS or to hold spacewalking astronauts as they carry out more complicated jobs on distant parts of the station. Two other robots are oddjobbers. Dextre performs routine tasks on the outside of the ISS, such as changing batteries or connecting cables. Its arms are tipped with multitools such as a wrench, drill, light and camera. Robonaut works inside the ISS, wiping down handrails to avoid dirt getting into the air, checking air flow from vents and other tasks.

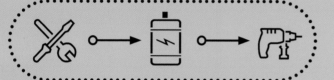

TECHNOLOGY TALK

Canadarm2 and Dextre have inbuilt motion and force sensors. Computers in the arms are programmed to monitor and control how much the arms move and how much force they use based on messages sent from these sensors. This means, for example, that the astronauts controlling the arm can 'feel' how hard it touches or grabs things, and avoid overtightening and damaging nuts and bolts.

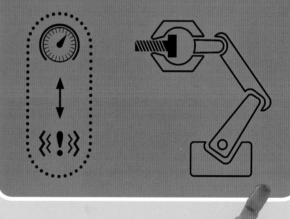

Robonaut is a humanoid robot with robotic arms tipped with gripping, dextrous hands. Its feet can clasp objects rather like a monkey's.

SPACE SHUTTLES

COLUMBIA, THE FIRST SPACE SHUTTLE, WAS LAUNCHED IN 1981. IT WAS USED TO TRANSPORT ASTRONAUTS AND SUPPLIES BETWEEN EARTH AND THE ISS UNTIL 2011, WHEN NASA ENDED THE SPACE SHUTTLE PROGRAMME TO FOCUS ON OTHER PROJECTS.

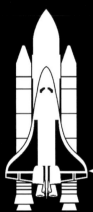

The main part of a shuttle was the orbiter, which looked like a plane, where astronauts lived and worked. The orbiter was launched from Earth with a blast from its main engine, plus pushes from two solid rocket boosters. These boosters then dropped into the ocean and could be reused. A large, orange external fuel tank attached to the orbiter fuelled its trip into orbit. Once empty, the tank dropped off and burned up on entering Earth's atmosphere.

TECHNOLOGY TALK

When returning spacecraft get closer to Earth, gravity's pull makes them speed up. Hitting the atmosphere creates friction between speeding metal and air. This friction produces air resistance that helps to slow the craft, but also enough heat to raise temperatures high enough to melt and burn metal. Discarded rocket stages are left to burn up. Space shuttle orbiters were covered with thousands of tiles made from materials that were not only insulating but also reflected heat. They could withstand temperatures of up to 1260°C.

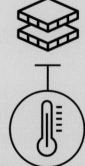

The space shuttle was 56 m tall with an orbiter that was 37 m long. The orbiter part of the shuttle was left in orbit around Earth. It could use its engine to slow down and its 14 thrusters to change direction to dock with the ISS, for example. The orbiter delivered astronauts to the ISS to work and launched satellites into orbit. When it was time for ISS astronauts to return to Earth, the orbiter flew down like a plane, gliding to land on a runway. Then it could be prepared to fly on another mission.

ROBOTIC ARM

CARGO HOLD

CARGO

DOORS

Large doors on the shuttle opened to load and unload its cargo, with the aid of a robotic arm.

The orbiter used a tough parachute to increase air resistance and slow down when landing on a runway. Then it could be prepared to fly on another mission.

AIRCRAFT TYPE WINGS

ROCKET ENGINES

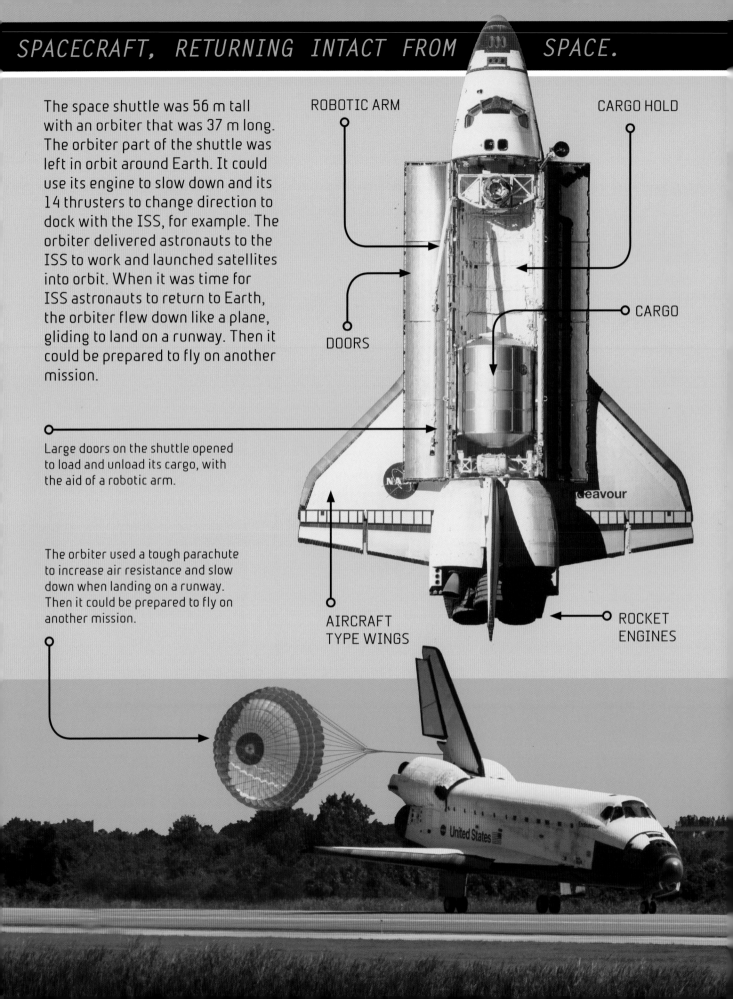

SINCE THE DAWN OF SPACE EXPLORATION, SCIENTISTS, TECHNOLOGISTS AND ENGINEERS HAVE COME UP WITH A VARIETY OF AMAZING SPACECRAFT THAT HAVE HELPED HUMANS TO EXPLORE SPACE.

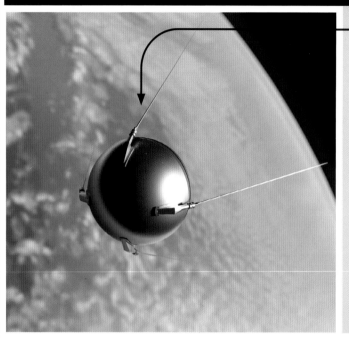

SPUTNIK 1

Sputnik 1 was the first spacecraft to orbit the Earth on 4 October 1957. It was a simple artificial satellite about the same size as a basketball. It was launched by the Soviet Union, and its name is Russian for 'travelling companion'. Sputnik 1 circled Earth every 96 minutes until early 1958, when it fell back and burned up in the Earth's atmosphere.

APOLLO 11

Apollo 11 was the first spacecraft to land men on the Moon. It launched from Florida, USA on 16 July 1969 using a Saturn V rocket. Apollo 11 had a command module, where astronauts stayed for the flight, and a lunar module, which they used to explore the Moon's surface.

MIR SPACE STATION

The Russian space station Mir was the first space station. It was assembled in orbit from 1986 to 1996, around 15 years before the ISS (see page 20). Travelling at an average speed of 28,783 kph, Mir orbited about 400 km above Earth for 15 years. Astronauts aboard Mir grew the first crop of wheat from seed in space!

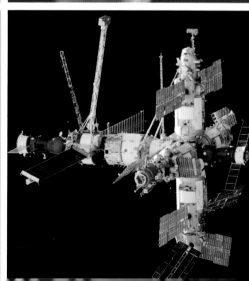

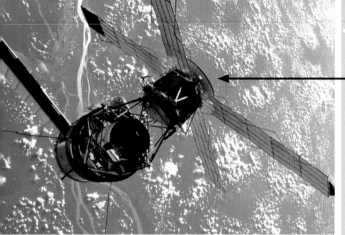

SKYLAB

Skylab was the first US space station, launched into Earth's orbit on 14 May 1973. Skylab was 30.2 m long and 6.7 m in diameter. After being visited by three crews, it started to degrade in the Sun's rays. In July 1979, it entered Earth's atmosphere and broke up, pieces of it falling into the Indian Ocean and across Australia.

SPACE SHUTTLE *CHALLENGER*

NASA had five space shuttle orbiters: *Atlantis, Challenger, Columbia, Discovery* and *Endeavour. Challenger* first launched in 1983 and made over ten missions, including that which took the first female US astronaut, Sally Ride, into space. It is sadly most famous for its final mission in January 1986, when a booster seal failed and hot gas burned through the external tank, causing a fatal explosion that killed the seven astronauts on board.

SPACEX DRAGON V2

The 7.2-m-tall SpaceX Dragon V2 is designed to carry astronauts to Earth's orbit and beyond. The first Dragon has been carrying cargo to and from the ISS since 2012, but Dragon V2 has a capsule that can carry both cargo and seven passengers into space. It can land almost anywhere on Earth, refuel and fly off again rapidly.

SPACE TELESCOPES

ASTRONOMERS USE POWERFUL OPTICAL TELESCOPES ON EARTH TO VIEW STARS AND PLANETS, BUT CAN GET A FAR CLEARER VIEW BY ...... USING SPACE TELESCOPES THAT BEAM BACK THEIR REMARKABLE VIEW.

The night sky is rarely dark on Earth because of light pollution from street lights, homes and cars. This makes dimly-lit distant objects in space harder to spot. Our atmosphere is also made from moving air that bends or refracts the light from space so objects are less clear. This is the reason why stars appear to twinkle. These effects are reduced by building observatories on high ground in places with less light pollution, or by making telescopes that use special mirrors to reduce the refraction of light from space.

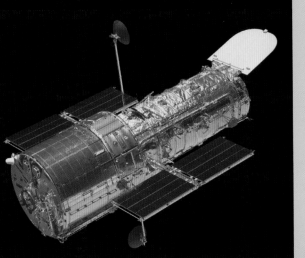

Hubble has been observing the far reaches of space from 569 km above Earth since 1990.

In space, however, telescopes can get a clearer shot of everything because there is no light pollution. Space telescopes, such as the Hubble Telescope, detect not only visible light, but also invisible light including ultraviolet and infrared. Other space telescopes can even detect the faint X-rays produced by galaxies billions of light years away. Images are sent back to Earth from space telescopes as data signals that are reconstructed into images by powerful computers.

SCIENCE TALK

Warm objects such as the Sun give off infrared light, or heat. The clearest way to view stars and planets far away is by using the infrared they emit, rather than visible light. Scientists have devised sensors on space telescopes that can detect even tiny amounts of infrared radiation. Such technology is useless on Earth's telescopes because the atmosphere absorbs most of this radiation.

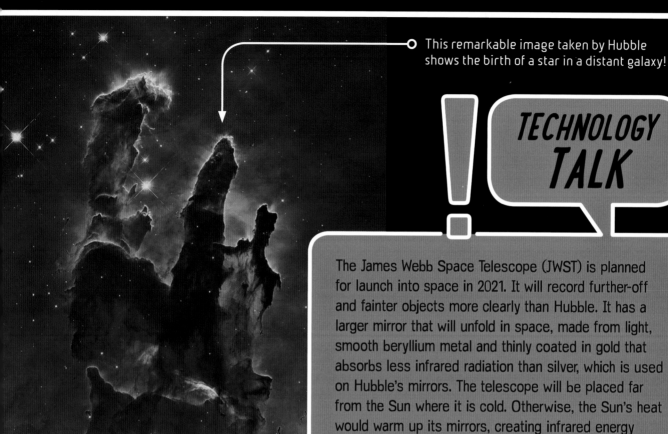

This remarkable image taken by Hubble shows the birth of a star in a distant galaxy!

TECHNOLOGY TALK

The James Webb Space Telescope (JWST) is planned for launch into space in 2021. It will record further-off and fainter objects more clearly than Hubble. It has a larger mirror that will unfold in space, made from light, smooth beryllium metal and thinly coated in gold that absorbs less infrared radiation than silver, which is used on Hubble's mirrors. The telescope will be placed far from the Sun where it is cold. Otherwise, the Sun's heat would warm up its mirrors, creating infrared energy that would conceal the faint radiation from other galaxies that the telescope is trying to detect.

MATHS TALK

Hexagons are shapes that fit together without gaps. They occur naturally in wax honeycombs made by bees to raise their young, but are also used in the JWST's mirror segments. Individual motors tilt each mirror by amounts as small as thousandths of a human hair's thickness to focus light exactly onto the JWST's sensors.

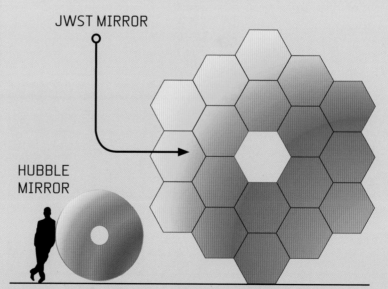

JWST MIRROR

HUBBLE MIRROR

OVER TIME, PEOPLE STUDYING SPACE HAVE DISCOVERED MORE AND MORE ABOUT THE AMAZING SPACE PHENOMENA FOUND IN THE UNIVERSE.

BLACK HOLE

A black hole is an area in space where gravity is so strong that even light cannot escape. Gravity is so powerful in a black hole because a lot of matter is compressed into a small space, for example, such as when a star dies and collapses in on itself. Black holes themselves are invisible, but scientists can see their effects.

DWARF PLANET

A dwarf planet is a huge, spherical, natural object that orbits the Sun just like other planets. But it is much smaller. Dwarf planets are generally less than a third of the diameter of Earth. Pluto is a dwarf planet that was considered a full planet until 2006. Then, experts reclassified it as a dwarf planet because they found its gravity was too weak to pull smaller nearby objects towards it, which is a requirement for a planet.

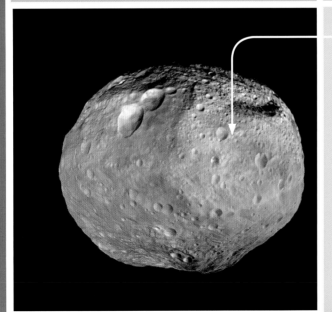

ASTEROID

Asteroids are rocks up to 600 km wide that orbit the Sun, but are too small to be called planets. These were left over from the Big Bang 4.5 billion years ago (see page 4–5). About once a year, an asteroid as big as a car enters Earth's atmosphere, ignites into a fireball and burns up before reaching Earth's surface.

METEROID

Meteoroids are fragments of space rock that orbit the Sun. Most meteoroids burn up in a flash of light, sometimes forming a meteor shower, when they enter Earth's atmosphere. People often call them 'shooting stars'. Any meteoroids that hit Earth are called meteorites. Once every 2,000 years or so, a meteorite as big as a football field touches down somewhere on Earth! This can create massive craters and throw up giant dust clouds.

COMET

A comet is a gigantic ball of ice, dust and rock that orbits the Sun. If it strays too close to the Sun, the ice inside it condenses into gas. This forms the glowing tail we see in the night sky when a comet passes over. Many comets take hundreds or thousands of years to orbit the Sun, and very rarely pass near Earth. The famous Halley's comet is a more regular visitor, appearing every 74–79 years!

SUPERNOVA

A supernova is the explosion of a star. It is the largest explosion that happens in space. A supernova creates so much light that it can burn brighter than a whole galaxy of stars and it releases more energy than our Sun will in its entire lifetime. Supernovas are important because they release matter such as carbon and iron throughout space. Almost everything on Earth is made up of these materials.

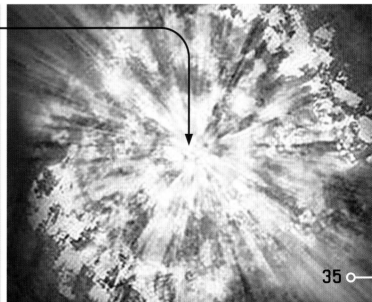

PROBES AND ORBITERS

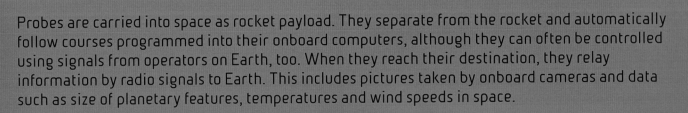

PROBES ARE ROBOT VEHICLES THAT TAKE ONE-WAY TRIPS TO COLLECT SCIENTIFIC INFORMATION FROM THE UNIVERSE. ORBITERS ARE LIKE PROBES BUT ARE DESIGNED TO ORBIT PLANETS OR MOONS TO STUDY THEM IN GREATER DETAIL.

Probes are carried into space as rocket payload. They separate from the rocket and automatically follow courses programmed into their onboard computers, although they can often be controlled using signals from operators on Earth, too. When they reach their destination, they relay information by radio signals to Earth. This includes pictures taken by onboard cameras and data such as size of planetary features, temperatures and wind speeds in space.

This is an artist's impression of the Voyager 1 probe. The two Voyager probes have travelled continuously since launch in 1977 at speeds of 57,000 kph, sending data about space back to Earth.

SCIENCE TALK

The Voyager probes are the most distant spacecraft from Earth. They are over 110 AU away and are reaching interstellar space, the gap between the solar system and other galaxies. Scientists keep in touch with these and other distant spacecraft using the Deep Space Network. This is a set of giant antenna dishes that can detect weak radio signals. The radio signals from the Voyager probes are 20 billion times weaker than the battery of a digital watch.

Cameras on the Cassini orbiter took this incredibly detailed image of Saturn's rings in 2013.

Orbiters circle near planets multiple times to take sequences of close-up images that show changes such as volcanic eruptions and shifting cloud patterns. Their sensors collect detailed data, such as the chemical composition of atmospheres around other planets. Probes and orbiters have discovered some amazing things. For example, Jupiter has over 60 moons, some with active volcanoes on their surface, and Saturn has wind speeds of over 1,700 kph.

THINKING OUTSIDE THE BOX!

Probes and orbiters travelling to destinations near the Sun use solar panels to produce power to move and run their instruments. But vehicles visiting the outer gas planets are moving away from the Sun, where the Sun's strength is weaker. Therefore, engineers install engines on these vehicles that convert the heat from nuclear power packs into electricity. Then they can carry on working in the darkness of space.

MATHS TALK

Mathematicians help probes and orbiters reduce travel time by calculating ways for them to hop between planetary orbits. Planets have different sizes and speeds of orbit around the Sun. It makes sense to time the trip for when they have moved closest together. A spacecraft to Mars, for example, can loop several times around Earth, accelerating faster and faster using gravity. Then, at a precisely calculated time, it exits this orbit at speed to meet up with Mars' orbit. This process is called gravity assist.

LANDERS AND ROVERS

PROBES AND ORBITERS GO CLOSE TO OBJECTS IN SPACE, BUT LANDERS ACTUALLY TOUCH DOWN ON THEM. SOME CARRY VEHICLES CALLED ROVERS DESIGNED TO EXPLORE THE OBJECT AFTER ARRIVAL. BOTH ROBOTIC MACHINES HELP PEOPLE ON EARTH TO KNOW MORE ABOUT SURFACE CONDITIONS ELSEWHERE IN THE SOLAR SYSTEM.

Landers need to be tough to survive the descent. They may have to pass through poisonous or searingly hot atmospheres around planets such as Mars and then reduce speed from very fast to a standstill without crashing. Landers gain as much information as possible about the area they land in. For example, they use robotic arms to scoop up soil, which they test for the chemicals it contains. Cameras take detailed images of the surface to help them map features such as hills, craters and valleys.

SkyCrane was a lander that lowered the rover Curiosity to the surface of Mars. It hit Mars' atmosphere at 21,000 kph and used air resistance, a parachute and downward-pointing thrusters to slow down to just 2.4 kph. Then it lowered Curiosity safely to the surface on ropes, before flying away and self-destructing.

PROJECT

Design a lander to carry a delicate object, such as an egg, from up in the air down to the ground without damage.

- What system(s) would you use to slow the descent?
- Which material could cushion the landing?
- How could you protect the object inside from high or low temperatures?

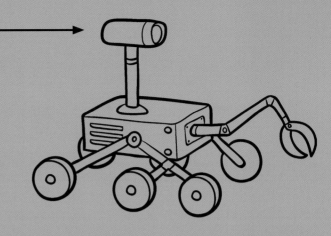

Rovers get images and data from a much wider area than landers, as they can move around. They often transmit data to their lander which may be orbiting the planet and which can communicate with Earth. These tough motorised vehicles vary in size from a microwave oven to a car. Some are steered using signals from Earth but others navigate themselves.

The first rover was driven by astronauts on Moon missions. Today's rovers are robots that move automatically across other planets and even comets.

TECHNOLOGY TALK

Operators on Earth send map references of rover destinations but a rover's onboard computer calculates the best route by comparing images taken by its cameras with stored maps and necessary data. If it meets unexpected obstacles, operators calculate and transmit the best route, but the rover also learns how to deal with similar problems for the future. Engineers use similar technology to develop smarter driverless vehicles on Earth.

"MATHS TALK

In 2014, the Philae lander touched down on a speeding comet. The spacecraft carrying it (Rosetta) had left Earth in 2004. Mathematicians had to calculate where the comet was going to be ten years ahead of time, and spot a landing opportunity. Philae took seven hours to land after release from Rosetta and its speed was very carefully controlled. If its speed had been out by just 1 cm each second, then it would have been over 252 m off target, and could have fallen off the comet!"

CURIOSITY

CURIOSITY IS THE MOST ADVANCED ROVER EVER BUILT. SINCE LANDING ON MARS IN 2012 (SEE PAGE 38), THE DATA IT HAS COLLECTED HAS HELPED SCIENTISTS GET ALMOST FIRST-HAND KNOWLEDGE OF THE PLANET.

Curiosity is the size of a small car. On top, there is a mast with cameras so scientists on Earth can see where it is going and what it is doing. It has a laser to blast rocks and sensors to detect what chemicals they contain. If they are of interest to scientists, operators command Curiosity to stretch out its robotic arm to collect a sample to analyse in more detail.

Curiosity's 2015 selfie shows the rocky terrain of the large Mars crater where it landed. It is still exploring that crater to this day.

ENGINEERING TALK

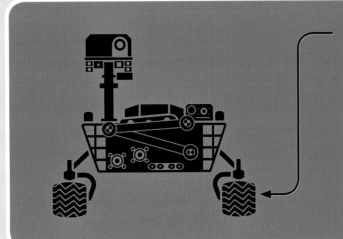

Curiosity is engineered to cope with the dusty soil and bumpy terrain of Mars. It has six large wheels with thick treads or grooves to increase friction. Each wheel has its own motor to move the rover in all directions. It also has a suspension system so springy that Curiosity can drive over obstacles 1 m high (twice as high as its wheels) while keeping all six wheels on the ground for stability.

A dried up ancient lake on Mars.

SCIENCE TALK

One of Curiosity's tasks is to look for signs of life on Mars. Until 2014, there was no evidence. But then Curiosity sampled whiffs of methane in the atmosphere. This gas contains carbon, which is a substance most living things contain. Curiosity also unearthed carbon-rich chemicals in sandy rocks on the planet. The carbon could have come from space dust, but on Earth, this gas is usually made by living things called bacteria. Could this be proof of life at last on the red planet?

ART TALK

David Hockney and other artists have produced photomontages or images made from lots of overlapping photos. Each is taken from a slightly different viewpoint and combine to create a different image than one produced from a single viewpoint. Mars teams have constructed wide-angle 'selfie' views of Curiosity and its terrain in a similar way by piecing together dozens of different photos taken by a camera on its arm.

Tools in Curiosity's arm tip include a grinder to drill holes in rocks, a spectrometer to test quantities of chemicals in rocks and a microscope for close viewing. Other sensors onboard are like artificial noses to check the gases in the atmosphere. Curiosity moves very slowly and methodically in its work. Its top speed is just 0.14 km/h, so it won't travel across the whole planet any time soon!

PROJECT

Produce a self-portrait using a montage of overlapping photos of your face.

■ Try using some close-ups and some wide-angle shots from varying viewpoints.

■ Think of how you could show the passage of time or family resemblances in a photomontage.

SPACE COLONIES

THERE ARE MANY REASONS WHY PEOPLE HAVE EXPLORED SPACE SO FAR, PRIMARILY KNOWING MORE ABOUT THE UNIVERSE AND LOOKING FOR SIGNS OF OTHER LIFE. THIS QUEST WOULD HAVE BEEN IMPOSSIBLE WITHOUT CUTTING EDGE SCIENCE, TECHNOLOGY, ENGINEERING, ART AND MATHS SKILLS TO SOLVE PROBLEMS. NOW PEOPLE ARE USING THEIR KNOWLEDGE OF SPACE TO PLAN FOR THE NEXT STEP: HUMAN COLONIES ON OTHER PLANETS.

Our planet is perfect at supporting life as we know it. It has an oxygen-rich atmosphere, a range of temperatures that living things can cope with, supplies of water and other natural resources. However, demand from an increasing human population is putting pressure on these resources and causing other problems, such as pollution.

Probes, orbiters and rovers have proven that Mars is the nearest planet most resembling Earth. It is rocky, has ice and other signs of water and its rocks contain mineral resources, such as iron, which is useful for building. However, the atmosphere is mostly choking carbon dioxide, it is colder than Antarctica and it has planet-wide dust storms. Technological solutions will be needed to melt Mars' ice for drinking water, produce oxygen from its atmosphere and warm colony buildings enough to grow plants for food. But life on Mars may one day be possible.

TECHNOLOGY TALK

Mars is over 56 million km away but the furthest people have travelled from our planet is around 400,000 km. With current rockets, a human mission to Mars would take about nine months each way. The enormous weight of the launch vehicle, lander, fuel, crew, water and other life support for a complete mission is at least seven times greater than even the newest heavy-lifter launch vehicles could carry. So the only solution is to construct and take supplies to the Mars mission craft while it is in orbit.

The Space Launch System includes a rocket and the Orion spacecraft. This new system can lift 130 tonnes of cargo. It is planned for use from 2021. Orion will be eventually used for a test trip to Mars and back to Earth, kickstarting a new era of Mars exploration.

THINKING OUTSIDE THE BOX!

Towering termite mounds are constructed by millions of insects coordinating their efforts to make single complex structures. Scientists are being inspired by this cooperation in developing mini robots capable of digging and constructing in teams on Mars and other planets. For example, if one robot places its brick in one location, the next uses visual clues and its programming to put its brick next to it, on top of it or elsewhere that helps build the final construction.

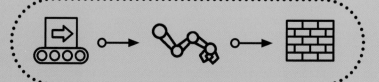

SPACE TOURISM

SPACE TRAVEL IS USUALLY RESERVED FOR HIGHLY TRAINED ASTRONAUTS, BUT A NEW WAVE OF NEAR-SPACE SPACESHIPS COULD BE TAKING TOURISTS TO SPACE IN THE VERY NEAR FUTURE.

In the next few years, space tourism companies hope to start taking paying passengers beyond Earth's atmosphere. Fully trained astronauts would fly the spacecraft, taking tourists on a trip lasting about 90 minutes, up to 160 km above the Earth. Here, the tourists will experience several minutes of weightlessness and a clear view of the stars above and planet Earth below.

TECHNOLOGY TALK

Space tourism is currently only really an option for the super-rich, but new technology will allow anyone to view the wonders of space from their armchair. A satellite with wide field-of-view cameras and sensors will beam high-definition live images of space and Earth to virtual reality headsets.

One company working with the Russian national space agency has already taken passengers for ten-day trips to the ISS, at a cost of over US $20 million each. Now private companies are testing new tourist spaceship designs. Virgin Galactic's SpaceShipTwo is a reusable, winged spacecraft that is designed to repeatedly carry up to eight people, including two pilots, into space. Anyone who takes such a flight automatically receives official astronaut status.

SpaceShipTwo doesn't launch from the ground like most rockets. It is carried up to over 15,000 m by a jet aircraft. It then ignites its rocket engine and takes off on its own.

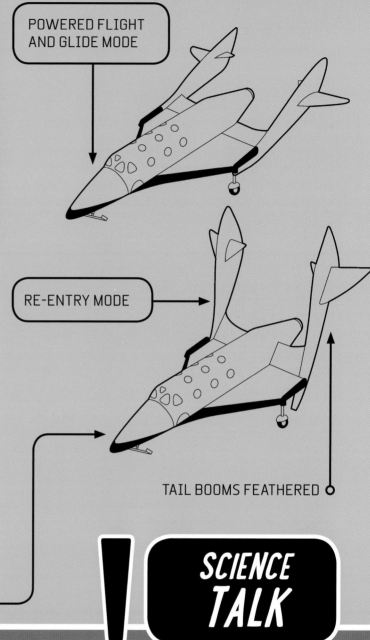

POWERED FLIGHT AND GLIDE MODE

RE-ENTRY MODE

TAIL BOOMS FEATHERED

THINKING OUTSIDE THE BOX!

SpaceShipTwo can work like a space capsule or a winged vehicle at different times during its flight. To safely re-enter Earth's atmosphere, it can reposition its wings. The tail booms move from a horizontal position to a 65-degree upright angle. This is known as feathering and it helps to slow down the spacecraft during its descent. The tail booms return to their normal position so SpaceShipTwo can glide down to land on a runway.

SCIENCE TALK

A lot of fuel is burned at rocket launches, emitting carbon dioxide. The gas and soot emitted by the rockets store the Sun's heat and warm the atmosphere. This global warming is raising average temperatures on Earth, contributing to changing weather patterns and melting polar ice. Increased global warming and climate change could be a consequence of increased space tourism in future.

GLOSSARY

aerodynamic describes something that has a shape that reduces air resistance

air pressure the push of air on the surface of objects

air resistance the force of air that slows down moving objects

asteroids large chunks of rock in the solar system

atmosphere blanket of gases around a planet

bacteria microscopic living things

black hole a place in space with such a powerful gravitational pull that even light cannot get out

carbon dioxide a gas in the atmosphere that is linked to global warming

comets objects in space made of ice, water dust and gases

drag another name for air resistance

escape velocity the speed that an object needs to be travelling to break free of a planet or moon's gravity

force a push or pull upon an object resulting from the object's interaction with another object

friction the pushing force that slows objects down when they slide against each other

galaxies huge systems of stars, dust and gases held together by gravity

GPS (Global Positioning System) a system that uses signals from satellites in space to locate positions on Earth

gravity a force pulling objects with mass together

helium a gas that is lighter than air

insulation a material that stops heat or cold passing through it

laser a narrow, concentrated and very powerful beam of light

mass the measure of how much matter is in an object

microgravity very weak gravity that creates a feeling of weightlessness

observatory a room or building that houses a space telescope

orbit the path one object in space takes around another

orbiter unmanned spacecraft that flies in orbit around a planet collecting images and data

oxygen gas in air that living things need to breathe in order to live

payload cargo carried to space on a rocket

probes unmanned spacecraft used to explore and record space

propulsion the force that moves something forwards

radiation energy in the form of waves or particles

refract to bend light

satellite electronic devices or bodies, such as the Moon, high in space that move around Earth

sensors devices that detect and measure something, such as amounts of a particular gas in the air

Soviet Union a former union of countries in Eastern Europe that included Russia

space station a large spacecraft that remains in orbit

streamlined shaped to reduce air resistance and move through the air easily and quickly

thrust a force usually produced by an engine to push a vehicle forwards

thruster an engine that creates thrust by expelling a jet of fluid or gas

X-rays a type of radiation that can pass through most materials

FURTHER READING

How Things Work in Outer Space Paul Mason (Wayland, 2018)

Our Universe Kevin Wood (Wayland, 2018)

Journey into Space Michael Bright (Wayland, 2018)

WEBSITES

FIND OUT MORE ABOUT SPACE AND SPACECRAFT:

Learn about the universe at **www.esa.int/kids/en/learn/Our_Universe/Story_of_the_Universe/What_is_space**

Games about our solar system https://spaceplace.nasa.gov/solar-system-explorer/en/

See the position of all the satellites at **www.stuffin.space**

QUIZ

- Who invented the first rocket?
- Why can some spacecraft not run on solar power?
- What is gravity assist?
- Who was the first human in space and who was the first to walk on the Moon?
- Why do space telescopes get clearer images of the universe than telescopes

INDEX

QUIZ ANSWERS

- Robert Goddard
- They are too far from the Sun to get enough light
- Moving around one planet using its gravity to orbit and build speed to jump to another orbit
- Yuri Gagarin and Neil Armstrong
- There is less light pollution, atmospheric interference and absorption of infrared radiation